P9-DMO-489

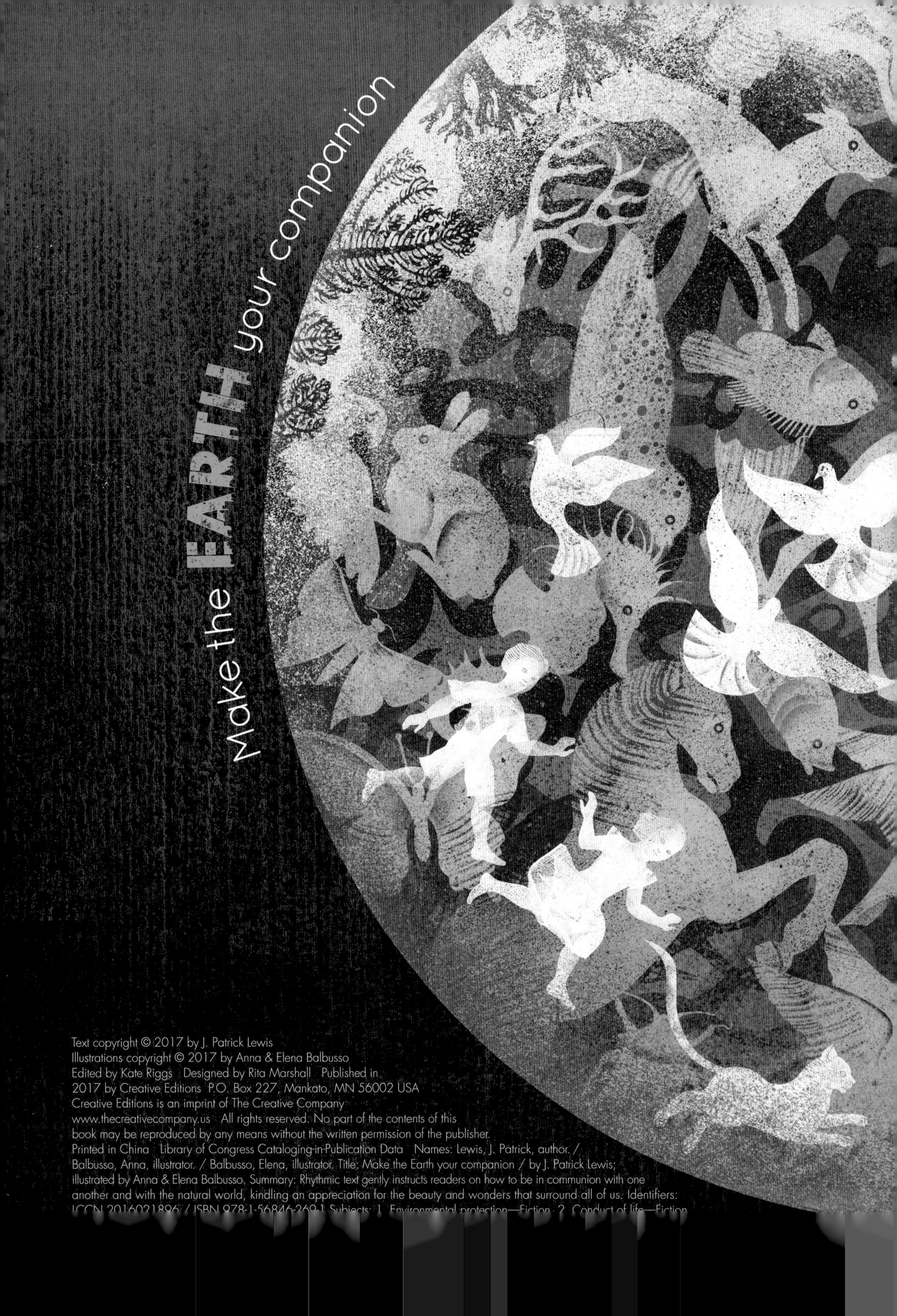

Edited by Kate Riggs Designed by Rita Marshall Published in
2017 by Creative Editions P.O. Box 227, Mankato, MN 56002 USA
Creative Editions is an imprint of The Creative Company
www.thecreativecompany.us
Printed in China Library of Congress Cataloging-in-Publication Data Names: Lewis, J. Patrick, author. /
Balbusso, Anna, illustrator. / Balbusso, Elena, illustrator. Title: Make the Earth your companion / by J. Patrick Lewis;
illustrated by Anna & Elena Balbusso. Summary: Rhythmic text gently instructs readers on how to be in communion with one
another and with the natural world, kindling an appreciation for the beauty and wonders that surround all of us. Identifiers:
LCCN 2016021896 / ISBN 978-1-56846-269-1 Subjects: 1. Environmental protection—Fiction. 2. Conduct of life—Fiction

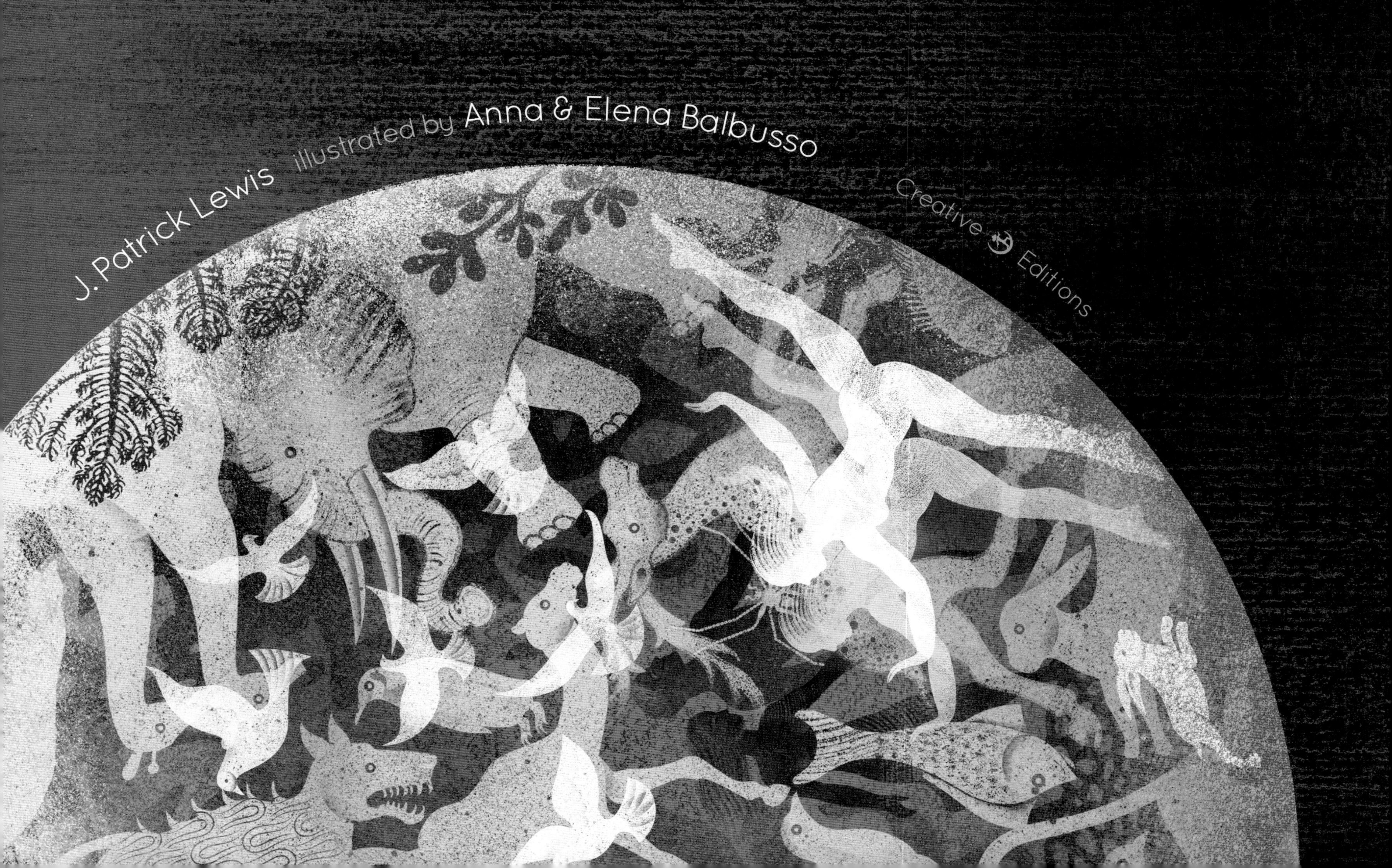
J. Patrick Lewis
illustrated by Anna & Elena Balbusso
Creative Editions

Make the EARTH your companion.

Walk lightly on it, as other creatures do.

Let the **SKY** paint her beauty—

she is always watching over you.

Learn from the SEA
how to face harsh forces.

Let the **RIVER** remind you that everything will pass.

Let the **LAKE** instruct you in stillness.

Let the **SPRING** reveal
the Earth at its rebirth.

Let the **MOUNTAIN**
teach you grandeur.

Let the WOODLAND
be your house of peace.

Let the RAINFOREST

be your canopy of hope.

Meet the **WETLAND**
on twilight ground.

Save some small piece of **GRASSLAND** for a red kite on a windy day.

See the **ICECAPS** glisten
with crystalline majesty.

Hear the **DESERT** whisper
hush to eternity.

Feel the **TOWN** weave a
small basket of togetherness.

Make the EARTH your companion.

Walk lightly on it, as other creatures do.